The tone is established from the outset: wry, wise, sardonic and playful, drawing the reader irresistibly in. Solonche is revealed as a philosopher in the mould of Wittgenstein: aphoristic, charismatic, acerbic and oddly mystical. If you met this book in a bar, you would definitely want to take it home with you and every day thereafter congratulate yourself on how lucky you've been. But that is true of all his books.
— David Mark Williams

The best feature of Solonche's poetry is its diversity. Everyone who encounters this volume (including the postman who delivers it to you) will find something in it to understand and remember – and a great deal to enjoy.
— Tony Beyer

"Solonche is productive and prolific, but that doesn't water down his poetry… He can compress a philosophical treatise into three lines… His epigrammatic tidy poems are philosophic gems. Solonche sees humor and encapsulates it; he frames a thought in perfect verse… He's playful and profound — the more he writes, the more he seems to know. Beneath the Solonche simplicity are significant social comments, and his goodwill reinforces the best in us."
— Grace Cavalieri,
Washington Independent Review of Books

In a style that favors brevity and pith, J.R. Solonche brings a richness of experience, observation, and wit into his poems. *Here is the world!* they exclaim. *And here, and here, and here!*

Watched over by ancient lyric gods – Time, Death, and Desire – we find the quotidian here transformed.
— Christopher Nelson,
editor of Green Linden Press

J.R.Solonche's many books of poetry, one nominated for a Pulitzer Prize, reveal a wry and vivid wit, a sharp but sympathetic eye, and a respect for the homely but significant detail, all wedded to an acute social and cultural consciousness. In his imaginative progress through city streets and country roads, the commonplace becomes the extraordinary… In lines full of mischief or romance, gaiety or grief, he is the poet of the every day, spent on earth or in an imaginary heaven.
— Judith Farr,
author of *What Lies Beyond: Poems* and
The Passion of Emily Dickinson

YEARS LATER

Years Later

A collection of poems

by

J.R. SOLONCHE

Adelaide Books
New York / Lisbon
2021

YEARS LATER
A collection of poems
By J.R. Solonche

Copyright © by J.R. Solonche
Cover design © 2021 Adelaide Books

Published by Adelaide Books, New York / Lisbon
adelaidebooks.org

Editor-in-Chief
Stevan V. Nikolic

All rights reserved. No part of this book may be reproduced in any manner whatsoever without written permission from the author except in the case of brief quotations embodied in critical articles and reviews.

For any information, please address Adelaide Books
at info@adelaidebooks.org
or write to:
Adelaide Books
244 Fifth Ave. Suite D27
New York, NY, 10001

ISBN: 978-1-954351-98-1

Printed in the United States of America

Books by J.R. Solonche

The Dust
A Guide of the Perplexed
For All I Know
The Moon Is the Capital of the World
Piano Music
Enjoy Yourself
The Time of Your Life
The Porch Poems
To Say the Least
A Public Place
True Enough
If You Should See Me Walking on the Road
I, Emily Dickinson & Other Found Poems
The Jewish Dancing Master
Tomorrow, Today, and Yesterday
In Short Order
Heart's Content
Invisible
Won't Be Long
Beautiful Day
Peach Girl: Poems for a Chinese Daughter (with Joan I. Siegel)

Contents

Books by J.R. Solonche **7**

I Saw All of Them **15**

The Attire of the Frequent Flier Screamed Esquire **17**

He Was Already There Before I Was There **18**

Orpheus **19**

Echo and Narcissus **20**

Such a Thing **21**

Like Father Like Daughter **22**

The Cardinal in the Corner **23**

There Are Fourteen Mirrors **24**

O, Give Us the Aberrants! **25**

I Didn't Go This Morning **26**

I Imagined I Could Remember **27**

A Bitter Harvest Is Better than None **28**

Phantom Limbs **29**

Ice *30*

The Sky *31*

Magnolia *32*

Wisdom *33*

The Sun and the Shadows Are My Companions *34*

Cupid and Psyche *35*

1825 *36*

A Private Plane *37*

There Is a Hole in Your Secret *38*

I Am Waiting for Heaven to Stop Falling *39*

Liquid Mind *40*

Three *41*

So Now *42*

The Sound of Green *43*

Morris Karp *44*

The Jonah Story *46*

Diary of 56 Days in an Israeli Psychiatric Hospital *47*

Often I Wonder *49*

There Should Have Been Another Myth *50*

I Know the Crocus *51*

Unhappily Never Before *52*

It Was a Beautiful Day *53*

YEARS LATER

What Does the Wind Want Me to Say *54*

Early March *55*

Two Spiders *56*

Positively Negatively Capable *57*

They Were Talking About the Universe *58*

There Are Two Flags There *59*

The Shadow *60*

Sale *61*

I Went There *62*

The Lone Rangers *63*

Swamp *64*

Yellow *65*

I Want to Be *66*

There Was a Tuesday That Wanted to Be Yesterday *67*

It's All About the Sky *68*

The Story *69*

Under the Leaves *70*

Birdhouse *71*

Going Nowhere, Son *72*

Obverse Observed *73*

I Took the Feeder Down *74*

Cold Snap *75*

The Whirlwind   *76*

Warm Afternoon   *77*

Flag   *78*

High School   *79*

Swans   *80*

Mourning Doves   *81*

Stricken   *82*

Years   *83*

Sonnet   *84*

Seasonal   *85*

Sonnet   *86*

The Jet   *87*

Echo   *88*

The Trees Must Know   *89*

The Clouds, the Sun, the Trees, the Rain, the Wind   *90*

The Word Wore White   *91*

The Sun, the Sky, the Mourning Dove   *92*

I Want to Be Wanted Dead or Alive   *93*

Punctuation Is All   *94*

Conversation   *95*

The Crocus   *96*

A Wish   *97*

YEARS LATER

Office Hour **98**

Conundrum **99**

Dialogue **100**

After the Reading **101**

I Followed the Sun **102**

The Sky **103**

Every Neighborhood **104**

A Race Against Space **105**

Thanksgiving **106**

Believe Me **107**

Them **108**

Saint Stone **109**

A year **110**

Emphasis Is All **111**

In My Dream **112**

Years Later **113**

My Last Poem **114**

About the Author **115**

I Saw All of Them

I saw all of them.
I saw all of them going off.
I saw all of them going on the highways.
I saw all of them lying low, not wanting to be seen.
I heard all of them.
I heard all of them lying.
I heard all of them telling the truth when it suited them.
I saw all of them in their suits of silver and gold.
I saw all of them in their pantsuits of platinum.
I saw all of them in their sweaters of species endangered.
I saw all of them in their scarves of scarcity.
I saw all of them in their shoes of extinction.
I heard all of them smirk into their wrists.
I heard all of them cackle into the airy ears of nowhere.
I heard all of them swear.
I saw all of them walk through the door
    held open by the doormen.
I heard the doormen curse in their own
    language so no one could hear.
I saw their teeth flash like neon at night.
I saw their eyes shine and glow, one of silver, one of gold.
I heard their lips suck the milk of diamonds.
I heard the soft hum of the handshake.
I heard the swift whish of whisky.
I heard the tight tinkle of ice.

J.R. Solonche

I saw the deal of the dead.
I saw all of them head for the exits.
I heard all of the earth exhale in all its languages.
I saw all of the earth head for the exit.

The Attire of the Frequent Flier Screamed Esquire

I wanted to stick out my leg.
I wanted to trip him.
I wanted to trip him up.
I wanted to ruin his trip.
He had a big mustache.
He had a big wallet with much cash.
He paid for a bagel
and coffee with a hundred dollar bill.
He took no change.
He left it all as tip.
Bless his soul.
But still.
But still I wanted to ruin his trip.

He Was Already There Before I Was There

He was already there before I was there.
He was already singing.
He was already seated in his solid silver chair.
But I got there just in time.
But just in time I was singing just in tune.
But just in time I pulled up a silver plated chair.
I was always the next to tallest.
I was always the next to best.

Orpheus

Orpheus, your lyre was a liar.
It couldn't tell truth if it wanted to.
And you know it didn't want to.
You know it didn't know how to.
What for?
Orpheus, Orpheus, Orpheus.
That's all I hear.
You make me nervous.
O, Zeus, free us from this Orpheus!

Echo and Narcissus

Echo and Narcissus,
for all we know,
could have been Narcissus and Echo.

They could have danced all night
by the light
of the silvery moon.

Echoism is not a crime.
Narcissism is not a crime.
Did the punishments fit?

What's so bad about
being a flower?
What's so bad about it, about, about

a flower,
a flower,
a fucking flower?

Such a Thing

What kind of man would say such a thing?
"Such a Thing," the man said.
Such a Man would say such a thing.

What kind of man would think such a thing?
"Such a Thing," the man thought.
Such a Man would think such a thing.

What kind of man would do such a thing?
"Such a Thing," the man did.
Such a Man would do such a thing.

What kind of man would believe such a thing?
"Such a Thing," the man believed.
Such a Man would believe such a thing.

Like Father Like Daughter

"What a noise from down
the hill. Sounds like two
chainsaws. What the hell
is my neighbor doing?
Cutting down every tree
on his place?" I thought this
this morning, so I went down
the hill to see what the hell
he was doing, and sure enough,
there they were, the two
of them, both with chainsaws
screaming bloody murder,
him and his dumb daughter.

The Cardinal in the Corner

I stole that idea.
I stole that idea of the corner.
I stole that idea of red.
I stole that idea to put red in the corner.
I looked for red.
I found a red pen and put in the corner.
I looked for red.
I found a red dishtowel and put it in the corner.
I looked for red.
I found a red coffee mug and put it in the corner.
I looked for red.
I found a red pillow and put it in the corner.
I looked for red.
I found a red silk rose and put it in the corner.
No matter what I did, I could not make
    the cardinal in the corner.
But I like the idea of red in the corner.
I will keep the idea.
It is a good idea.

There Are Fourteen Mirrors

There are fourteen mirrors.
I counted them.
I wanted to know.
So I counted them.
There are wall mirrors.
There are stand mirrors.
There are hand mirrors.
There are rectangular mirrors.
There are oval mirrors.
There are round mirrors.
There is one concave mirror.
There is one full-length mirror.
There is no convex mirror.
This means I cannot write a self-portrait in a convex mirror.
Fourteen mirrors are many mirrors.
Fourteen mirrors are thirteen too many mirrors.
All you need for a fairy tale is one honest-to-goodness mirror.

O, Give Us the Aberrants!

And we shall nail one to our doors.
And we shall wear one around our necks.
And we shall bronze one like our baby shoes.
And we shall frame one within silver.
And we shall wrap one in linen.
And we shall emblazon one upon our banners.
And we shall emboss one upon our shields.
And we shall incise one into the steel of our swords.
And we shall weave one into the clothes of our cause.
And we shall brand one upon the stainless
    flesh of our foreheads.

I Didn't Go This Morning

I didn't go this morning,
so I spent the morning not going.
I didn't do it this afternoon,
so I spent the afternoon not doing it.
I didn't hear it this evening,
so I spent the evening not hearing it.
But this morning was well-spent.
And this afternoon was well-spent.
And this evening was well-spent.
All day, all day, I got my money's worth.

I Imagined I Could Remember

I imagined I could remember the moon
    was whispering in silver.
I imagined I could remember the orange
    mountain losing light.
I imagined I could remember the double
    voice of the two winds.
I imagined I could remember the flag
    struggling to be free of the pole.
I imagined I could remember the smell of
    the salt air through the garden.
I imagined I could remember the way the
    porpoises were one with the waves.
I imagined I could remember the way the waves were wavy.
I imagined I could remember the beach
    bleached as the blondes.
I imagined I could remember the way the gulls
    waved wings goodbye, goodbye, goodbye.

A Bitter Harvest Is Better than None

I have eaten bitter bread.
Would you rather I starve?

I have eaten bitter fruit.
Would you rather I go hungry?

I have drunk bitterness directly from the bitter well.
Would you rather I die of thirst?

Would you?
Would you really?

Phantom Limbs

I used to have two lilacs.
They died.
They are no more.
Yet still I smell lilac in the yard.
But this is only when I close my eyes.
But this is only when I inhale too deeply for
    the breath of ordinary breathing.

Ice

The ice thawing
on the lake sings
as it turns back
to water again
a song neither
happy nor sad,
but just a simple
wordless tune
for going home.

The Sky

The sky, mostly blue,
but not entirely,
is nevertheless
a pure sky for whom
the clouds do not diminish
but replenish
with timorous temerity
its integrity.

Magnolia

I can already see,
even now in February,
how magnanimous
the magnolia is going to be.
I can already see
it will give away thousands,
thousands so magnificently!

Wisdom

Some sort of fly
flew over from some
place and landed
on the book I was
about to read,
then washed its hands
of it and flew off.
I read the first page
and did the same thing.
Smart fly.

The Sun and the Shadows Are My Companions

The sun and the shadows are my companions.
They have nothing in common.
They are not on speaking terms.
They use me as their intermediary.
The sun said, "Tell the shadows…"
So I told the shadows what the sun said.
The shadows said, "Tell the sun…"
So I told the sun what the shadows said.
This went on until the clouds showed up.
The clouds did not need me to speak for them.
The clouds spoke directly to the sun and to the shadows.
The clouds said, "Shut up."
So the sun shut up.
So the shadows shut up.
So I shut up.

Cupid and Psyche

Cupidity and Psychology
fornicated on a cloud,

and that's how the twins
Cupidology and Psychidity were born.

1825

It was a good year.
John Quincy Adams was president.
This house was built.
It's still here.

A Private Plane

A private plane
passed overhead.
It couldn't be seen.
It was overcast.
It was exactly
the sound I expected
gray to be.

There Is a Hole in Your Secret

There is a hole in your secret.
It is a very small hole.
It is the circumference of a small pin.
It is lets your secret leak out slowly.
It lets your secret leak out so slowly you cannot hear it.
But if you put your ear right up against it, you will hear it.
It says, "Shhh."
It says, "Can you hear me?"
It says, "Do not tell."
It says, "I am a secret."
It says, "Shhh."
It says, "Can you hear me?"
It says, "Shhh."

I Am Waiting for Heaven to Stop Falling

O, heaven is falling!
Where will the angels go?
Where will the angels live?

They cannot live here.
They cannot live on earth.
They will not know how to live here with us.

O, heaven is falling down!
Where will the angels go?
Where will the angels live?

They will not be welcome here.
We will not welcome them here.
We will build a roof against them.

O, heaven is falling!
O, the rest of the angels are falling!
Let us build a roof over our heads to keep off the angels!

It is of the angels I am thinking.
It is of the angels, not of us.
It is of the angels.

Liquid Mind

I have arthritis.
I have sciatica.
The pills weren't working.
The exercises weren't working.
The medical marijuana wasn't working.
I went to the acupuncturist.
She put on music.
It was flute.
It was relaxing.
It was called "Liquid Mind."
She put needles in my back.
I didn't feel the needles.
She triggered the muscles.
I felt the muscles jump.
She had liquid hands.
She had a sense of humor.
She told me to drink lots of water.
I asked her if I could drink bourbon with the water.
She said I could.
I said I would write a poem about her.
She laughed.
She had a liquid laugh.
Like I said, she had a sense of humor.
On my way home, I stopped at Hennessy's Liquor.
I asked for a fifth of "Liquid Mind."
Never heard of it, he said.
It's a new whiskey, I said.
I'll order it, he said.
Don't bother, I said. It doesn't work.

Three

My cat died.
My neighbor's dog died.
My other neighbor's wife died.

Someone's cat was born.
Someone's dog was born.
Someone's wife was born.

Everything happens in threes.
So it is said.
So they say.

So Now

So now it's all
positioning,

the time
for timing it right,

the down-closing,
the in-drawing.

So now it is
up to the sleepers,

all the lucky sleepers
whose sleep

will never
need a dream.

The Sound of Green

It sounds the green sound of water.
It sounds the green sound of wind.
It sounds the green sound of song birds.
It sounds the green sound of insects with wings.
It sounds the green sound of insects without wings.
It sounds the green sound of the child
   all the way down the road.
It sounds green.
The sound of green sounds green.

Morris Karp

Morris Karp was born in Russia.
Morris Karp was the father of my mother.
Morris Karp came to America in 1910.

Morris Karp spoke only Russian
Morris Karp learned English in America.
Morris Karp got a job operating a
   sewing machine in America.

Morris Karp made pockets for businessmen's
   jackets in America.
Morris Karp made pockets for
   businessmen's coats in America.
Morris Karp knew injustice in America.

Morris Karp did not know the word *injustice*.
Morris Karp was active in the union of garment workers.
Morris Karp fought for a 40-hour week.

Morris Karp fought for decent conditions of work.
Morris Karp fought for a living wage.
Morris Karp was beaten by a police officer on the street.

Morris Karp showed me the scar he got in America.
Morris Karp showed me the perfect pockets
   he made for businessmen in America.
Morris Karp told me something.

YEARS LATER

Morris Karp told me how he learned the
    difference between *tear* and *tear*.
Morris Karp said, *A tear is a tear in your eye.*
Morris Karp said, *A tear is a tear in your pocket.*

The Jonah Story

I do not like the Jonah story. The Jonah story
    is all obedience and disobedience,
God calling on the wind to frighten the
    sailors, God calling on the whale
to swallow up Jonah and spit him out again on
    dry land, God calling on the worm
to desolate the vine. The Jonah story is all
    God calling. I do not like the way
the Jonah story ends. The Jonah story ends
    without ending. It ends with God asking
Jonah a question, but really asking one of those
    holy rhetorical questions that God is
so fond of, and that is where Jonah is left
    hanging, on the question mark of God.
And I do not like this because I want to know
    what happens to heroes at the end of
stories. What happens to Jonah at the end of his
    story? What does Jonah do? Does he
go home? Does he stay where he is on the east
    side of Nineveh where he prepares a
field of gourd vines? Does he sleep twenty-
    four hours through? Does God leave
Jonah alone? Does God leave Jonah alone,
    finally, finally, in the shade of the vine?

Diary of 56 Days in an Israeli Psychiatric Hospital

And on the first day
they stared at him
as he shaved and he showered
And on the second day
one introduced himself to him
and he had scars on both wrists
and they stared at him
as he shaved and he showered
and they gave him bitter cigarettes
and they gave him breakfast
And on the third day
he taught himself
to smoke the bitter cigarettes
they gave him before breakfast
and the one with scars on both wrists
showed him the rope-burn on his throat
and they stared at him
as he shaved and he showered
And on the fourth day
another one introduced himself
and he asked him for a bitter cigarette
and he had skin like goat's milk
and eyes like the blue sky
and he asked him if he were an angel
and he said that yes he was
and he asked him if he would fly for him

and he said that yes he would
and they stared at him
as he shaved and he showered
And on the fifth day
he played chess with a Polish poet and lost
and at noon he flew for the one
with the skin like goat's milk and the eyes like the sky
and when he came back to earth
he asked him for three bitter cigarettes
and they stared at him
as he shaved and he showered
And on the sixth day
the one with the scars on both wrists
and the rope-burn on his throat
showed him a picture of his mother
and they no longer stared at him
as he shaved and he showered
And on the seventh day
the one with skin like goat's milk and eyes like the sky
asked him for all his bitter cigarettes
and the one with scars on both wrists
and a rope-burn on his throat and the picture of his mother
asked him to teach him how to fly
and he said that yes he would
he would teach him how to fly
for all his bitter cigarettes
Walk around the room seven times
and seven times chant the foregoing

Often I Wonder

Often I wonder what I would
have done had I been there.
Would I have tried to run
through the back of the house
or leaped out of a window
or hidden in the coal bin?
Would I have fought with them
and been killed right there on
the step of the front door, right
then in the middle of the night?
Would I have gone obediently
without a murmur? Later, at
the train, would I have grabbed
under an arm for a gun, hoping
to take at least one? Or later in
the cattle-wagon, would I have cut
open a vein in my wrist with the lens
of my glasses I would have broken?
Finally, in the camp, would I have
starved myself by giving my bread
to another man? I never wonder if
I would have lived. That would be a sin.

There Should Have Been Another Myth

A myth is missing.
There never were enough.
There has always been a space.
It has always been a chasm too wide to cross.
There has always been a burning question.
It has always burned the tongue.
There has always been the gaping gap between the hills.
It has always been impossible for the moon to fill.
A myth is missing.
It should have been.
It should have been meant to explain the future.
It should have been meant to explain the origin of failure.
It should have been meant to explain how fire begat desire.
A myth is missing.
There should have been one more.
There should have been one more behind the temple door.
Certainly a myth is missing.

I Know the Crocus

I know the crocus.
I know the white crocus.
I know the purple crocus.
I know the orange crocus.
I know when they will come up.
I know where they will come up.
I know what I will say.
I will say, "Welcome."
I will say, "Welcome to the upper world."
I will say, "You are the first."
I will say, "Forgive us."

Unhappily Never Before

They danced down the aisle.
They sang up the smile.
They danced more than a mile.
They sang without guile.
They danced without style.
They sang in single file.
They danced and danced and danced before the trial.
They sang and sang and sang all the while.

It Was a Beautiful Day

"It's a beautiful day," I said.
"It's the kind of day that makes life worth living," I said.
"As opposed to what?" Jim said.
"All those other kind of days that don't?
Those overcast days?
Those damp and rainy days?
Those raw and icy days that cut to the bone?
Those sleet days?
Those dark days?
Are those the kinds of days that don't make life worth living?"
You have to understand.
Jim teaches philosophy.
One must be careful about what one says
    to one who teaches philosophy.

What Does the Wind Want Me to Say

What does the wind want me to say
flipping the pages
of the notebook so furiously,
or does it want me to put down the pen
and speak for itself?

Early March

See what Mars
has to do with it.
Winter is at war
with spring.
The champion
of warm and
the champion
of cold, the sun
and the wind,
in single combat,
and we know
which will win,
if not today, soon.

Two Spiders

Whitman's is fine.
It's noiseless.
It's patient.
It's the soul of a poet.
Nothing wrong with that.
But Dickinson's is better.
It crawls around her ass.
It chases her from the outhouse.
It's the body and soul of a poet.
It's so much better.
That's so much better.

Positively Negatively Capable

The odes are not for me.
The sonnets are all right.
But my favorite is "La Belle Dame sans Merci."
I knew one once who had me in thrall.
She was more than all right.
Alas, she was not for me.
That's all.

They Were Talking About the Universe

They were talking about the universe.
So I listened to them carefully.
The universe interests me.
So I listened quite carefully.
The only other thing that interests me as much is poetry.
So when they talk about poetry, I listen carefully,
So far I have not heard them talk about the universe as poetry.
If they ever do, I will listen carefully.
I will listen very, very carefully.

There Are Two Flags There

There are two flags there.
One flag has stripes of red and white.
It has white stars upon a field of blue.
The other flag has a snake chopped up in pieces.
The chopped up snake is upon a field of yellow.
The yellow is a garish yellow.
The chopped up snake has a rattle on its tail.
There is a motto.
The motto reads, *Don't tread on me.*
The first flag has no motto.
Perhaps it should have had a motto.
Perhaps it should have been, *Forgive me.*

The Shadow

of the book
looks like
a crow
on the patio
stones but
tells nothing
of what
it knows,
if it knows
anything
besides looking
like it does,
as it were,
so this is why
it is known as
the trickster.

Sale

I had my eye on
the broken scythe
in the corner of the barn,
covered in cobwebs
next to an old churn.
I asked him how much.
It's not for sale he said.
How did it break?
I asked. Did he strike
a stone while harvesting
the wheat? No. He broke
it against a tree while
remembering his high school
sweetheart. It's not for sale,
he said again. Is it all
right if I write a poem
about it? Sure, he said.
Somebody should, I guess.
Thanks, I said. He smiled.
Then waved, more or less.

I Went There

I went there because that is where the silver is.
I went there because that is where the angels dance on pins.
I went there because that is where the
    moon flies off the handle.
I went there because that is where the stars light up their lips.
I went there because that is where the
    mountains mount the snowy horses.
I went there because that is where the
    roses rise to prominence.
I went there because that is where the lilies are most at ease.
I went there because that is where the rain marries the rivers.
I went there because that is where the
    ghosts of the sunsets are.
I went there because that is where the
    saints go to hide their sins.
I went there because that is where you
    go to live 40 years selfishly.
I went there because that is where you
    go to live 40 years selflessly.
I went there because that is where you
    go to mean what you say.
I went there because that is where it
    means more than anything.

The Lone Rangers

Who was that asked man?
Who was that basked man?
Who was that casked man?
Who was that flasked man?
Who was that masked man?
Who was that tasked man?

Swamp

In the swamp,
the turtles
have arisen
from the bottom
mud to sun
themselves on
the big branches
of the dead trees
fallen from years
of turtles in
years of suns.

Yellow

The first yellow jacket
already knows how
to wear its yellow
jacket, for it was taught
how by the sun
in its mother's dream.

I Want to Be

I want to be
out here when
the first honey bee
comes out here.
I want to see
it find the cherry
blossoms on
the cherry tree.
I want to hear
its song of delight.
I want to see
the blossoms blush
with white
embarrassment.

There Was a Tuesday That Wanted to Be Yesterday

It waited on the second bench at the
    northeast corner of Second Avenue.
That was the plan all along for the second time.
It wore a red carnation.
It fed the pigeons.
It read *The Castle* for the second time.
It was the one you tried to forget for the second time.
You made Monday swear to silence.
You made Wednesday cross its heart and hope to die.
You promised them undying gratitude.
It was the Tuesday you wanted them to
    shoot for the second time.
The first shot to the chest missed.
The first shot to the head missed.
What's wrong with Monday?
What's wrong with Wednesday?

It's All About the Sky

It's all about how it is most of the earth.
It's all about how it is all around.
It's all about how it has many minds of its own.
It's all about how it can't keep a secret.
It's all about how it wears any color well.
It's all about how it is way above our heads.
It's all about how it birthed the birds.
It's all about how it spangles with stars.
It's all about how why it is blue.
It's all about how it is not a window.
It's all about how it is big in some places
    but not big in other places.
It's all about how it is Nut.
It's all about how it is Horus.
It's all about how we look up to it.
It's all about how it looks down on us.

The Story

It was so quiet today,
the only sound
was my neighbor's
washing machine
spinning a story
of falling over falls
head over heels.

Under the Leaves

Under the leaves
I blew off the walkway,
the worms wormed
their way out differently
from the way they
wormed their way in.

Birdhouse

Still filled with plenty
of past springs' worth
of twigs, the birdhouse
now has no room to house
this spring's worth of birds.

Going Nowhere, Son

Going nowhere, son,
is the same
as going everywhere,
which is the same, son,
as, eventually, going,
going, going, gone.

Obverse Observed

It is not so obvious
at first, the barbed
wire shadow, but
a minute into it,
you begin to make
out how the outline
falls in line around
the shadow in reverse,
oblivious to the ground.

I Took the Feeder Down

I took the feeder
down, but the squirrel,
undaunted, climbed
to the hook anyway,
and scratched whatever
suet was left behind,
then slid down, a furry
fantastical fireman.

Cold Snap

Yellowing, the forsythia
have not foreseen it,
this spring cold snap,
but the daffodils,
holding in abeyance
their yellow still
still below, have.

The Whirlwind

The whirlwind hoists
the dried leaves
fallen from fall
then coughs them up,
rough, on the asphalt,
a dry cough, cough
in the whirlwind's voice.

Warm Afternoon

An insect,
once hidden inside
from the insecticide
outside, comes out
to see what the fuss
is all about. That sound,
imperceptible,
is its shout.

Flag

Flailing first, then flung out on the wind,
my neighbor's flag
flaps on one wing perpendicular
to its pole,
a filibuster of red, white, and blue.

High School

Her name was Deirdre.
She had blonde hair.
She had blue eyes.
She dropped her book at my feet.
I picked it up.
I handed it to her.
I said, "My fault."
I walked down the hall.
I did not look back at Deirdre.
I did not look back at Deirdre's blonde hair.
I did not look back at Deirdre's blue eyes.
It was my fault.
It was all my fault.
All, all, all was my fault.

Swans

My neighbor Eva likes
to watch the swans
that live on the lake.
She says it's funny how
they're so majestic
with their long, graceful
necks in the water while
on land, they waddle
around on those short legs.
She says she's embarrassed
for them. Listen, Eva, I say,
don't be silly. Evolution
made them exactly that way
for a reason, for goodness
sake. They're paddles, which
are perfect for life on a lake.
Well, I don't like it, she says.
They look stupid. They do,
I say. But only one third
of the time. When flying
and swimming, perfect bird.
Their glass is two-thirds full
and one-third empty. Ours
at best is half and half.
At least, that made her laugh.

Mourning Doves

For some reason,
the mourning of
the mourning doves
does not sound as
sad in the morning
as their mourning
in the afternoon.
This must be because
my mood is darker then.

Stricken

I am struck
by how many times I'm stuck
in thought's same place.
It's as though someone is out to get me,
someone who will never show his face.

Years

A bonsai forest,
the moss of decades
cascades over
the whole stone wall
to nearly cover it.

Sonnet

You wanted to say something before it was too late,
so why didn't you before it was too late say something?

You wanted to go while there was still time,
so why didn't you while there was still time go?

You wanted to make up for lost time,
so why didn't you for lost time make up?

You wanted to find the right time,
so why didn't you the right time find?

You wanted to take it all back,
so why didn't you it all back take?

You wanted to stop it from happening,
so why didn't you it from happening stop?

You wanted it to stop right then,
so why didn't it, why didn't it, why didn't it right then stop?

Seasonal

The green struggles
against brown's own world
and brown's abettor, cold,
which together hold
their claim to the place
as long as the sun
cannot decide which stays,
which goes.

Sonnet

What with one thing and another,
will we have to forego one thing or another?

While we watched one thing leave with another,
would we have to forsake one thing to have another?

If only one thing could take the place
    in our hearts of another,
should we hold to one thing only and
    with the other not bother?

What if the one thing could only sing,
and the other only dance?

What if the one thing is the one and only brass ring
while the other is the one and only chance?

What if one thing is the father
while the other is the mother?

What if, with one thing and another,
one thing and another?

The Jet

The jet leaves
this sky over here
for that sky over there,
sucking in this sky over here
to leave in that sky over there.

Echo

Away in the woods
way off the road,
the pileated woodpecker
is the echo
of the motorcycle
that went down the road
just now.

The Trees Must Know

The trees must know.
I don't know how, but they must.
At least the wild cherry must know,
for look at how its two secondary trunks
rise up from its main trunk like arms upraised
to heaven, and how the larger branches
    are the palms of hands,
and how the smaller branches are the fingers of hands,
all asking, "Why?"

The Clouds, the Sun, the Trees, the Rain, the Wind

The clouds open and close.
The sun appears.
The sun disappears.
The sun reappears.
The trees sway in synchronous sway.
The trees dance in place.
The rain stays hidden in the clouds.
The rain wants to be a secret.
The wind wants to tell it all.
The wind wants to hold nothing back.
The rain holds its own.
The sun has nothing to be ashamed of.
The rain is patient and teaches patience by example.
The sun lets down its guard.
The sun lets you look.
The sun wears the mask of the moon and lets you look.
The trees are good at making you believe
    it is they who move the wind.
The wind is the ghost of the clouds.
The wind haunts the sky.
The wind punishes the trees for their insolence.

The Word Wore White

There was a wedding.
It was a private wedding.
No one was invited.
It was the wedding of the word.
The word was marrying the old man.
It was the word's first marriage.
It was the old man's second marriage.
The word was not a virgin.
The word slept with thousands of old men.
The old man was not a virgin but felt like one.
The word wore white.
The old man wore black.
The old man believed he was at a funeral.
It was a reasonable belief.

The Sun, the Sky, the Mourning Dove

The sun sings the old song
of the sky.

The sky sings the old song
of the mourning dove.

The mourning dove sings the old song
of the new mourning dove.

I Want to Be Wanted Dead or Alive

I want to be wanted dead or alive.
I want to be wanted like a bank robber.
I want to be desperate.
I want to be desperately wanted.
I want to be wanted like a desperado.
I want to be followed by the federales.
I want to be pursued by a posse.
I want to be tracked by an Apache tracker.
I want a reward on my head.
I want to see my face on posters on telephone poles.
I want to see my face on posters in post offices.
I want the reward to go up and up and up.
I want to be the hero of the pulp magazines.
I want to be the hero of the newsreels.
I want to be called a Robin Hood.
I want to be killed in a shootout with a dozen deputies.
I want my headstone to read: *He got
   what he wanted, dead or alive.*

Punctuation Is All

A cloud shaped
like a question mark questions
the facts of sky,
turning blue's exclamation
into *Why?*

Conversation

Jeff's wife has Alzheimer's.
Two or three times a week
she tells him to take her home.
They are home, of course,
but Jeff says all right. Get in
the car. I'll take you home,
he says. He drives the four miles
around the lake. We're home,
he says. Thank you, she says.
It's good to be home. Yes, he
says. It is. It is good to be home.
As I say, Jeff does this two or three
times a week. So far, so good,
he tells me. The human mind,
I say. The human mind, Jeff says.
It's amazing, I say. It's amazing.
Home is where the mind is. So far,
so good, Jeff says, looking at his feet.

The Crocus

While the crocus
are the first to come,
they are also the first to go,
so have the longest sleep
to another spring coming.
This is their blessing.
This is their curse.

A Wish

"We were born with the birth
 of the first hydrogen atom,
 and we shall die with the death of the last."
I don't know who said that, but I wish I had.

Office Hour

I don't understand this poem,
Mr. S., she said. Which one?
I said. "The King of Ice Cream"
by Steven Wallace, she said.
Okay, I said. Let's talk about
"The Emperor of Ice Cream"
by Wallace Stevens, I said.
Know what? I said. What?
she said. I don't understand
it either, I said. You don't?
she said. Nope, I said. But
you're the teacher, she said.
That's right, I said. I'm
the teacher, so now I'll
teach you something. Think
of the poem as a conversation
starter. A conversation starter?
Yes, Something that starts
a conversation. What you and I
are doing right now. You mean
having a conversation? That's
right. But we're having half
of the conversation. Go home
and have the other half of
the conversation with the poem.
Then come back, and we'll
continue our conversation.
Okay, she said. She didn't.

Conundrum

Someone spilled beer
in front of the grocery store.
I smelled its soulful sour
smell as I opened the door
of my car. It was under
the big banner
proclaiming, *Under
New Management.* I wonder
if it was intentional or
an accident, this spilt beer
in front of the grocery store.

Dialogue

The wild cherry says to the magnolia,
"Look, my leaves are more yellow than yours."

The magnolia says to the wild cherry,
"Look, my leaves last longer than yours."

After the Reading

"All appropriations are appropriate,"
he said. He was a famous poet, so
he knew what he was talking about.
"Not the same, which is different,
which is not the same," he said.
At this point, I was beginning to think
that famous poet or not, he didn't
know what he was talking about.
"To a poet, everything is a poem
except the poem," he said. Now
I was certain that the famous poet
did not know what he was talking
about. But I will say this. His poems
knew what they were talking about,
and isn't that all that matters?

I Followed the Sun

I followed the sun
around this afternoon.
I moved my chair
from the back to the side
to the front to stay in the sun.
I needed the sun that much.
I needed the sun that badly.
I needed the sun for that long.

The Sky

The jet leaves its contrail.
The red tail leaves its whistle.
I close my eyes.
I open my eyes.
I hear the contrail's whistle.
I see the red tail's contrail.

Every Neighborhood

Every neighborhood
needs its eccentric one.
Every neighborhood
needs its elderly gentleman
sitting in his driveway in the sun.
Every neighborhood
needs its poet who looks like
he's talking to himself but is talking to the sun.

A Race Against Space

Time has nothing to do.
Time is irrelevant.
Time remembers its childhood.
Time remembers the time it had space all to itself.
Time is bored.
Time rocks in its rocking chair.
Time twiddles its thumbs.
Time daydreams.
Time naps in the afternoon.
Time is tired.
Time needs to rest.
Time remembers the good times and the bad times.
Time opines if it only had world enough.
Time's favorite joke is why did the moron
    throw the clock out the window?
Time's favorite Yogi Berra story is You mean now?
Time's favorite time is Greenwich Mean.
Time's favorite people are those sentenced to life.
Time's favorite phrase is Time, gentlemen, time.
Time's favorite book is Ecclesiastes.
Time's favorite time piece is a Timex.
Time's favorite companion is the tide.
Time's favorite artist is Dali.
Time's favorite TV show is Howdy Doody.

Thanksgiving

The math of myth
is all it is.
They're all the same,
the holidays,
the holy days are wholly lies.
The math of myth
is all they are.
Each passing year
another layer
for the liar in you,
just another number
added to the math of myth.

Believe Me

It's hard to believe.
After today's warmth,
today's warm sun,
today's warm sunshine,
tomorrow will be sleet,
tomorrow will be freezing rain,
tomorrow will be cold on cold,
but as is true of everything,
everything gets harder and harder to believe.

Them

I heard them
in the branches' nation,
the bitter birds,
the agents of desperation.

I saw them
in the garden's creation,
the foul flowers,
the fools of sensation.

Saint Stone

Once a man
named Stone
had the plan
of his very own
to become a saint
by simply painting
his face and hands
with silver paint.
So he spent his fortune
on silver paint
and painted his face
and hands, and now
he is known
as Saint Stone
all over the place.

A year

I put out the pot
with last year's dirt.

It will make
this year's flowers.

How unlike last year's hurt.
How unlike this year's hours.

Emphasis Is All

Life is not
like that.

Life is like
that.

In My Dream

In my dream, I killed a flower.
It looked like a lily.
I punched it to death.
It turned into a pile of yellow gravel in a pot.
I tried to put the gravel back into a lily flower.
I was unable to.
I tried again but could not do it.
A third time I scooped the gravel up into a lily shape.
A third time the gravel stayed gravel in my hands.
I know this means nothing.
I never had a girlfriend named Lily.
The dream, nevertheless, troubled me for hours.

Years Later

Years later, the words were faded. The ink, once purple-black, was the ghost of brown. It was like the beech leaves scattered over the myrtle. The paper, once the white of cream, was the yellow-white of weathered paint, an old sailboat's hull. But beneath it, the photograph of the three of us was unchanged. It was still black and white. I was still stupidly self-conscious. You were still beautiful. He was still in front and between us, still slightly leaning into you. His face was still that haiku of eyes and mouth. Months later, spring came. Beneath the forsythia, the crocus appeared, head first. Some were purple. Some were yellow. Some were white. The rain was not icy anymore. The nebulous desires came into focus. The heart opened. It put forth its spike of fire. It burned purple. It burned yellow. It burned white. Weeks later, I remembered it. There was nothing more to learn by heart. There was nothing more to discover there. Two pleasures had to be enough, and they were enough. One pleasure had to be enough, and it was enough. Days later, the cloud shaped like a man in recline who has dreamed he has dreamed the three perfect dreams of the world, moved off on the wind. It revealed the moon. The moon was silent. The moon was silver. The moon was cold. The moon was the three perfect dreams of the world. Moments later, all was gone. The golden-yellow of the sun, the white of the clouds, the clear and endless blue of the sky were gone. All that was reflected in the window of the train was in the eyes and the mouth. The eyes blinked. The mouth opened. It was years later.

My Last Poem

It will be about spring.
I will write it in the dead of winter.

It will be dark pink in the middle.
It will be the exact color of magnolia blossoms.

Around its edges, it will be the precise white of wild cherry.
Or it will be the other way around.

This I will decide at the last moment.
A warm breeze will blow gently between the blank spaces.

It will be lifted up to be read.
Then the words will fall, slantwise, from the
    page into the palm of my hand.

There they will leave a fragrance, at once
    both familiar and unidentifiable.
No amount of water, nor any of prose, will ever wash it away.

About the Author

J.R. Solonche has published poetry in more than 400 magazines, journals, and anthologies since the early 70s. He is the author of *Beautiful Day* (Deerbrook Editions), *Won't Be Long* (Deerbrook Editions), *Heart's Content* (Five Oaks Press), *Invisible* (nominated for the Pulitzer Prize by Five Oaks Press), *The Black Birch* (Kelsay Books), *I, Emily Dickinson & Other Found Poems* (Deerbrook Editions), *In Short Order* (Kelsay Books), *Tomorrow, Today and Yesterday* (Deerbrook Editions), *True Enough* (Dos Madres Press), *The Jewish Dancing Master* (Ravenna Press), *If You Should See Me Walking on the Road* (Kelsay Books), *In a Public Place* (Dos Madres Press),

J.R. Solonche

To Say the Least (Dos Madres Press), *The Time of Your Life* (Adelaide Books), *Porch Poems* (Deerbrook Editions), Shelf Unbound 2020 Notable Indie Book, *Enjoy Yourself* (Serving House Books), *Piano Music* (nominated for the Pulitzer Prize by Serving House Books), *For All I Know* (Kelsay Books), *A Guide of the Perplexed* (Serving House Books), *The Moon Is the Capital of the World* (Word Tech Communications), *Selected Poems 2002 – 2021* (forthcoming in April from Serving House Books), and coauthor of *Peach Girl: Poems for a Chinese Daughter* (Grayson Books). He lives in the Hudson Valley.

www.ingramcontent.com/pod-product-compliance
Lightning Source LLC
Chambersburg PA
CBHW071420070526
44578CB00003B/637